How to Start, Run and Grow a Used Car Dealership on a Budget

Start Part-Time or Full-Time Right from Home

By

Aaron Simmons

Copyright © 2017 – **Valencia Publishing House**

All Rights Reserved.

No part of this publication may be reproduced, stored in a retrieval system or transmitted in any form or by any means, electronic, mechanical, photocopying, recording or otherwise without the proper written consent of the copyright holder, except brief quotations used in a review.

Published by:

www.Valenciapub.com

Valencia Publishing House
P.O. Box 548
Wilmer, Alabama 36587

Cover & Interior designed

By

Jasmine Carerra
First Edition

TABLE OF CONTENTS

Why Start a Used Car Dealership 5
What You Need to Get Started 8
    Business Organization 8
    Business Location 9
    Licensing 11
    Bond 11
    Sales Tax Requirements 13
    Staffing 13
State Regulations 14
Insurance 23
Licensing 29
        Credit worthiness and Personal Financial Statement 33
        Naming Your Business 35
        Incorporating Your Business 36
    Business Structure 37
    Sole Proprietor 38
    Partnership 38
    Corporation (Inc. or Ltd.) 39
        S Corporation 39
        Limited Liability Company (LLC) 40
        EIN Number from IRS 47
        Opening a Commercial Bank Account 49
        Required Forms and Documents 49
        Auction Houses 51
How to Get Started on a Budget 57

How to Get Financing 61
Legal Requirements 65
    Used Car Rule 66
    The Buyers Guide 69
Developing Your Inventory 82
How to Sell Cars 88
How Much Can You Make 92
    Front End vs Back End Commissions 94
    Make Money by Financing 95
How to Sell Used Cars Part Time from Home 98
Choosing The Best Dealer Software 106
How to Grow Your Used Car Dealership 112
5 Rapid Fire Q&A 115
Commonly Used Car Dealer Terms 118
Last Words 138

WHY START A USED CAR DEALERSHIP

Here are the three main reasons most people get interested in this line of business:

1. Barrier to entry is relatively easy
2. High-income potential
3. Not very time consuming

If you see the legal requirements, it is not hard to become a used car dealer even if you are on a tight budget. As far as the income potential is concern, it is higher than most other side gigs you find. Just imagine this, you buy a 6 years old Toyota Camry with 87K miles for say $4500, you bring it home, clean it up, fix few minor scratches, wash it wax it, then put it up for sale on Craigslist for $7100. In the first three days you get a few calls, and after 4 test drives, you sell it for $6600.

Let's see how much you made from this sale. You paid $4400 + you spend $350 on fixing minor issues, so your total cost was $4750, but you sold it for $6600, so your net profit from this sale is $6600-$4750 = $1850

Not bad for few hours of work. You see if you buy the right type of cars and price them right, there is no reason you can't sell 2-3 cars a month and make a handsome extra income each month.

I have a friend, who has a small insurance business. He has been selling cars on the side for last 25 years, and he told me just by selling 2-3 cars a month, he was able to pay for college for all his three kids.

On the other hand, if you want to grow, then start small but reinvest the profit you make from selling each car back into the business and soon you will see, you are growing at a fast and steady pace, but you have to be focused and dedicated.

Here are the 12 Steps You Need to Take to Get Started.

1. Apply and obtain appropriate surety bond

2. If a location is required by your state, get a location install appropriate signage
3. If required by your state, prepare a personal financial statement
4. If required, buy appropriate commercial liability insurance
5. Name your business
6. Incorporate your business
7. Get an EIN number from IRS
8. Open a commercial bank account
9. Apply and obtain your state auto dealer license
10. Apply and gain access to 2 major auction houses
11. Gather/Buy necessary Dealer documents
12. Start buying and selling cars

Let's discuss all these 12 steps first then we will get into the business and marketing aspect of the business.

WHAT YOU NEED TO GET STARTED

WITHIN the United States, there are two types of car dealers. There are new car dealerships that also market in used cars, and then there are independent used car dealers that focus entirely on pre-owned or leased vehicles. If you are going to consider selling used cars, there are a few things you need to get started.

BUSINESS ORGANIZATION

The first step in starting any business is to establish the proper business structure. If you aren't comfortable doing this on your own, you can hire a certified public accountant that knows the automobile business. An accountant can also help you with determining how much operating capital you need. You may also want to check with a commercial insurance agent with a background in liability and car dealership experience. You should go to your city or county clerk's office in order to get a business license and ask about other required local licenses.

BUSINESS LOCATION

If you are going to start your business from home, you may not need to look for a business location. However, in some states, it may be required of you to have a business location. Even if you are going to work from home, you may need to have specific layouts and requirements for your home based business.

If you are going to choose another location for your dealership you want to choose one that is visible and easily accessible from main roads. You'll obviously want a place with plenty of parking for your inventory and customer vehicles. You should always check with the local zoning office to make sure you can legally establish a car dealership at the location.

Here is what you can do to overcome this regulation. If you live outside the city limit, then chances are you are not subject to any city zoning laws. In most county, if you are not inside a neighborhood then you can make your home a business location and hang a sign. Check with your county zoning board. I did exactly that and made my home a business location. All I had to do is hang a sign with my dealership name and number took a picture of it and sent it to the state licensing board for approval.

If this does not work, check and see if you have a friend who lives outside the city and has a location where you can hang a sign and make that your business location. Remember if you are a small used car dealer, location is not as important, because when you carry 2-3 cars, it doesn't look like a dealership. Instead, you should rely heavily on local advertising. That is how I got started.

Now once you start to grow, yes, your location becomes more and more important. As you start to carry 20-50 cars or more yes then you will need a visible location with plenty of signs and lights, so your cars are visible from a distance and well-lit at night.

LICENSING

Next, you need to apply for your used car dealership license. Each state government has their own application process and requirements. Most require you to meet specific zoning regulations and go through a criminal background check.

You will likely also need to provide a surety bond in a specific amount required by the state. Once you complete the application process, you can likely expect an inspection by a state representative. Once everything is approved, then you will have your license to operate a used car dealership.

BOND

Typically the word bond can be confusing as there are investment bonds, government bonds, municipal bond and few others, but to fulfill your dealer licensing requirements you need to buy a surety bond, which is vastly different than any other types of bonds.

A used car dealer bond is a type of insurance that dealers must obtain before opening their business. The used car dealer bond protects customers against fraudulent or unethical actions by a dealer. The surety bond also assures potential customers that the dealer is financially secure.

The cost of this bond varies depending on your personal credit worthiness and your personal financial situation. But typically these bonds are sold through many local insurance agents, credit unions, commercial banks, or you can even do a search online for companies that sell these bonds nationwide.

If you have good credit, a typical $35,000 dealer surety bond will cost around $250.00/year, and it will have to be renewed every year. If you have less than perfect credit score, the cost will go up higher and maybe even double at times.

Here is a popular dealer site www.dmv.org where you can find more information about how to get a surety bond, follow the link below.

http://www.dmv.org/buy-sell/car-dealers/surety-bonds.php

SALES TAX REQUIREMENTS

All vehicles sold will require sales tax to be collected. This tax needs to be remitted based on your state's payment schedule. You can get a sales tax permit through your state's Comptroller of Public Accounts. They can also help you understand the procedure for collecting and paying vehicle sales tax.

STAFFING

Again, if you are starting the business out of your home you probably won't be hiring a lot of staff. Although in some states you will be required to have a trained repair person on staff or subcontracted. If you are going to hire any additional employees, you will need to contact the state Motor Vehicle Administration for individual licensing requirements.

If you are going to offer financing, you should hire a finance manager. Although when you first get started, you'll likely want to handle as many of the jobs as you can on your own.

STATE REGULATIONS

State	Requirements	Cost	Bond	Insurance	Other Requirements
Alabama	5+ vehicles sold in 12 months	$10	$25,000	Liability	Business License Permanent Location
Alaska	All dealers	$50	$50,000		
Arizona	4+ vehicles sold in 12 months	$115	$100,000		$22 background check fee per person
Arkansas	All dealers		$25,000	Liability	Location specifics
California	All dealers				Business License Resale Permit Used dealer

						training
						Location specifics
Colorado	3+ vehicles sold in 12 months		$50,000			Minimum net worth of $100,000
						Background check
						Credit Report
						Testing
Connecticut	All dealers	$560	$50,000			Location specifics
Delaware	5+ vehicles sold in 12 months	$100		Liability		Business License
						Location specifics
Florida	3+ vehicles sold in 12 months	$300				$54.25 per person application
						Training seminar
Georgia	All dealers	$170	$35,000	More than		Pre-license seminar

| | | | | | liability | Background check

Location specifics |
|---|---|---|---|---|---|---|
| Hawaii | 3+ vehicles sold in 12 months | $50 | $100,000 for >60 vehicles a month or $25,000 for <60 vehicles a month | | | A line of credit of $50,000 |
| Idaho | 5+ vehicles sold in 12 months requiring a title | $234 | $20,000 | | | $26 salesperson ID

Pre-licensing class |
| Illinois | All dealers | $1,000 | $20,000 | | Specific amounts required | Background check |
| Indiana | 12+ vehicles | | $25,000 | | | |

	sold in 12 months		0			
Iowa	All dealers					Location specifics
Kansas	All dealers		$30,000			3 credit references
Kentucky	All dealers	$140	$100,000	Specific amounts required		$20 salesperson license $20 background check Location specifics
Louisiana	All dealers	$30				
Maine	5+ vehicles sold in 12 months 3+ vehicles displayed in 30 days	$150				
Maryland	All dealers					
Massachu	All dealers	Not over	$25,00			

setts		$200	0		
Michigan	5+ vehicles sold in 12 months	$160	$10,000	20/40/10 no-fault fleet insurance	Registered repair facility or an agreement with a repair facility
Minnesota	5+ vehicles sold in 12 months	$285			
Mississippi	All dealers	$100	$25,000		Salesperson license
Missouri	6+ vehicles sold in 12 months	$150			Background check

Location specifics |
| Montana | All dealers | $30 | $50,000 | Liability | |
| Nebraska | All dealers | | $50,000 | Liability | $20 salesperson license

Location |
| Nevada | All dealers | $125 | | | $38.25 fingerprinting |

New Hampshire	All dealers	$125	$25,000		Criminal record check
New Jersey	All dealers	$100	$10,000	Specific amounts required	Location specifics
New Mexico	All dealers				Location specifics
New York	Buy with intent to resell Display 3+ vehicles in 1 month 5+ vehicles sold in 12 months	$748	$10,000 to $50,000		
North Carolina	All dealers	$90	$50,000	Liability	Licensing Course $20 salesperson ID
North Dakota	All dealers	$100	$25,000	Garage Liability	Location specifics $100

						inspection fee
Ohio	5+ vehicles sold in 12 months	$200				
Oklahoma	All dealers	$600				
Oregon	All dealers		$40,000	Liability		Education certificate
Pennsylvania	All dealers	$65	$20,000			
Rhode Island	4+ vehicles sold in 12 months	$302	$50,000			Repair service must be provided Approved credit line of $50,000
South Carolina	All dealers	$50	$30,000			Pre-licensing course
South Dakota	All dealers	$300	$25,000			
Tennessee	All dealers	$400				$35 salesperson license $200 show

							permit
Texas	All dealers						
Utah	All dealers	$127	$75,000				Orientation Course
Vermont	All dealers	$503					
Virginia	All dealers	$850	$50,000				$325 Dealer Course $50 Exam
Washington	4+ vehicles sold in 12 months	$975	$5,000				
West Virginia	All dealers	$150	$25,000				
Wisconsin	3+ vehicles sold in 12 months	$100 selling 12+ vehicles a month or $25	$50,000				

21 | P a g e

These regulations can help you see what you are up against in your state. Some are going to require higher fees while others are going to require more specific restrictions regarding the location and training.

If you are still interested in pursuing the start of a used car dealership, let's look into some of the specific things you need to do. To start, let's consider what you need when it comes to insurance.

INSURANCE

WHEN it comes to selling used cars, you are going to need insurance. Not only is insurance a requirement in most states, but it is also important to have insurance in order to protect yourself against problems that could impact your finances. The types of insurance that you will want to consider when starting to sell used cars include the following:

As you start you need to get:

➢ General Liability Insurance

Once you get established and growing, then you need to consider these following insurance:

➢ Workers Compensation(For your employees)

➢ Payment Protection Insurance

➢ Overhead Expense Disability Insurance

➢ Business Owner's Policy Group Insurance

It is important to know that there isn't a specific car dealership insurance coverage. It is important to have property and casualty coverage that can cover your fleet of vehicles. When you get insurance coverage be sure to check with the company to see if they offer a discount to a used car dealer. It is also a good idea to compare quotes from several insurance companies to make sure you are getting the best coverage for the best possible rate.

When you run a car dealership, you are going to be seeing cars come and go every day. As a result, you aren't able to insure each individual car. Even fleet insurance can be difficult. However, insurance is important since it will protect your business should one of the cars on your lot become involved in an accident.

All states require a registered vehicle to have car insurance. Cars at a dealership aren't registered with an owner, even though they are technically owned by the dealership. This means you need to purchase third party liability insurance at the least, which will include all the vehicles on your property. A dealership will typically need property and casualty insurance in order to get proper protection for all cars on the lot. These two insurance policies will cover things such as accidents, theft, fire, flood, etc.

When you are looking for insurance coverage you want to make sure your policy includes the following:

- ❖ Vehicles owned by customers while on your lot for repairs or maintenance.
- ❖ Loaner vehicles.
- ❖ Vehicles that aren't owned, but are listed in your system.
- ❖ Newly acquired vehicles that haven't yet been added to your lot.
- ❖ Accidents as a result of employees driving a lot vehicle.
- ❖ Accidents as a result of customers driving a lot vehicle.
- ❖ Accidents as a result of employees driving customer vehicles.

Most new car dealers make the mistake of assuming that private auto insurance is enough to cover accidents that occur from test drives. It is actually illegal for car dealers to have insurance specifically for a car lot.

When it comes to getting car dealer insurance, you won't be able to take advantage of discounts commonly available through private insurance such as driving history and vehicle type discounts. On the other hand, there are a few other discounts you can take advantage of when getting car dealer insurance.

If you do an extensive background check on employees, it will look better for insurance companies.

Some insurance companies provide a list of approved training courses for dealership employees that teach safety when dealing with customers and driving. Some insurance companies will also allow you to develop your own training program. Both of these options can provide insurance discounts for your dealership.

You can get a discount by sticking to a test drive route. This works by both decreasing the risk of accidents but also causes most insurance companies to offer a discount.

When you run a dealership, you have the option of running a driving background check on potential customers. If you make this a standard practice, then insurance companies will view you as a lower risk and reduce the cost of your insurance.

Lastly, you can secure your property and make it safe from theft. If you have added security features, you will get more discounts on your insurance. Some insurance companies will actually have specific security measure requirements to reduce your cost.

When you go to shop for car dealership insurance it is important to ask the following questions:

✓ How much insurance do you need?

✓ What discounts can you get?

✓ What premium options are available?

✓ Does your insurance company specialize in dealership insurance?

✓ How easily can you change a policy?

Here are the top 7 companies that specialize in offering auto dealer insurance.

1. Farmers
2. Federated
3. AIG
4. Zurich
5. Lexington
6. Scottsdale
7. Travelers

Once you have the appropriate form of insurance, then the next step is to get appropriate licensing. Let's take a look at the process for getting a dealership license.

LICENSING

SINCE you are planning to sell used cars you are going to need to get a car dealer license. Depending on the state you live in this can be a lengthy process and you are going to need to make sure you do it right. The first step in getting a dealer license is to do your research and find out what is required.

Refer back to the list under regulations to make sure you are even required to get licensed in your state. Some states only require you to get a license if you sell over a specific number of vehicles in a year. If you are still in doubt about whether or not you need a license then contact your local DMV for more information.

If you know that you need to get a license in your state, then you can contact the state authority and learn about the specific steps involved in getting your license. Each state varies greatly in their requirements and the process involved, so you should take the time to learn both the rules and the application process.

The state authority should be able to give you all the application forms you need. However, if they don't have what you need then take the time to download all the forms you need and read through them to see what you may need. Write down any questions you have before going to the state authority and getting things clarified.

Some applications are also going to require extensive information about your potential business that you'll need to research and have on hand before starting the application process. Even if there isn't a lot of information needed, the application forms can help you build a business plan.

Before you start filling out applications, it can be a good idea to go through a background check. Some states will require this process and others won't, but most bonding companies will require it. The background check will ensure you have a solid financial history or anything else in your past that can present a problem to starting a car dealership.

After you pass the background check, you can prepare a business plan. The business plan is essential for any business, even if you are going to be doing it from your home. For a used car dealership you want a business plan that is clear and well thought out to show creditors and licensing authorities that you are serious and committed. A business plan needs to have clear vision, goals, and objectives.

You'll also need detailed research on the market. You'll want detailed financial information for projected returns and costs.

In some states, before you get a car dealership license you need to first get a business license. You can visit your local city or county license commissioner's office to get this done.

Another requirement before starting a car dealership from your home is to apply for a surety bond. Most bond companies will give you a quote for free or a small fee. It is important that you have a good credit history and all your financial paperwork in place in order to get a surety bond. When you apply for a surety bond, you will need information about your business and the specific amount of bond needed. You'll then need to sign a credit release agreement.

You may also need to find a retail location (refer to the business location section). While you'll ideally be starting the business from home, in some states you are required to have a retail location that meets specific requirements. Some states only need proof of ownership, but others will require pictures and inspection so they can be sure you are meeting very specific requirements. Be sure to ask the state authority about the specific location requirements and then set about finding an appropriate location for your car dealership.

Lastly, you want to determine if you need to file incorporation papers. This is often only needed if you are going to file as a Corporation, Limited Liability Company or a Limited Liability Partnership. I will touch more on this little later.

CREDITWORTHINESS AND PERSONAL FINANCIAL STATEMENT

You should check your credit and know what's in it, know your Fico score, and if it is less than say 700, you need to find out why. Often, there are errors or a few minor late payments which you can file a dispute online with the credit bureau and get them taken care of.

As for the personal financial statement, this is a statement where you list all your assets and liabilities, and once you deduct your liabilities from your assets, whatever is left, that is your net worth.

Take a look at this sample personal financial statement so that you can get an idea, if you have an accountant, he or she can get this prepared for you, or you can download a template from online or send me an email at valenciapublishing@gmail.com and simply ask me to send you the financial statement format. I will email you a copy which you can fill out all on your own.

Personal Financial Statement of John Doe

1/1/2017

Assets	**Amount in Dollars**
Cash - checking accounts(2)	12,450.29
Cash - savings accounts(1)	46,231.10
Certificates of deposit	15,000.00
Securities - stocks / bonds / mutual funds	76,891.45
Notes & contracts receivable	17,321.63
Life insurance (cash surrender value)	28,531.00
Personal property (autos, jewelry, etc.)	197,451.88
Retirement Funds (eg. IRAs, 401k)	32,100.00
Real estate (market value)	312,000.00
Inventory Cash Value	28,700.00
Other assets (specify)	0.00
Total Assets	**766,677.35**

Liabilities	**Amount in Dollars**
Current Debt (Credit cards, Accounts)	14,765.14
Notes payable (Auto)	7,979.65
Taxes payable	4,155.12

Real estate mortgages (describe)	177,881.45
Other liabilities (HELOC)	0.00
Other liabilities (specify)	0.00
Total Liabilities	204,781.36
Net Worth	561,895.99

Signature:......................   **Date:**

NAMING YOUR BUSINESS

You need to come up with a name that is trendy, catchy and can be easy to remember. Along with the name you may also want to come up with a unique logo for your business. This is not the legal name, but your trade name.

For example, your company's legal name maybe ABC Investment LLC but your trade or DBA (doing business as) name maybe "Quality Cars of Eastern Shore" This is the name your customers will know and remember. So it is important that you pick a name that is easy to remember and reflects your business.

As for coming up with a logo, if you are like me, then I am sure you are not a creative guy and not good with computer graphics. But not to worry, there is a place on the web www.Fiverr.com where you can get a logo designed for $5. Hire a designer from there, explain to them what your business is and let them design a logo for you for $5.

INCORPORATING YOUR BUSINESS

When you choose a legal entity for your used car dealership there are two main factors to consider:

1. What you want

2. The type of business model you intend to build

Often you have the option of choosing to file as a limited liability company or LLC, general partnership or even sole proprietorship. A sole proprietorship is the ideal business structure for someone starting a used car dealership, especially if it is a moderate start from you home. However, most prefer the benefits of an LLC.

If you plan to eventually expand your used car dealership to other locations or potentially online, then you definitely don't want to file as a sole proprietor. In this instance, you should definitely file as an LLC.

When you file as an LLC, you will be able to protect yourself from personal liability. This means that if anything goes wrong while operating your business then only the money you invested into the company is at risk. This isn't the case if you file as a sole proprietor or a general partnership. LLCs are simple and flexible to operate since you won't need a board of directors, shareholder meetings or other managerial formalities in order to run your business.

Here are all the legal business structures you can choose from, it is best to get some advice from your CPA or accountant or an attorney.

BUSINESS STRUCTURE

When starting a business, there are five different business structures you can choose from:

- ✧ Sole Proprietor

- Partnership
- Corporation (Inc. or Ltd.)
- S Corporation
- Limited Liability Company (LLC)

SOLE PROPRIETOR

This is not the safest structure for an auto dealership business. It is used for a business owned by a single person or a married couple. Under this structure, the owner is personally liable for all business debts and may file on their personal income tax.

PARTNERSHIP

This is another inexpensive business structure to form. It often requires an agreement between two or more individuals who are going to jointly own and operate a business.

The partners will share all aspects of the business in accordance with the agreement.

Partnerships don't pay taxes, but they need to file an informational return. Individual partners then report their share of profits and losses on their personal tax returns.

CORPORATION (INC. OR LTD.)

This is one of the more complex business structures and has the most startup costs of any business structure. It isn't a very common structure among used car businesses since there are shares of stocks involved.

Profits are taxed both at the corporate level and again when distributed to shareholders. When you structure a business at this level, there are often lawyers involved.

S CORPORATION

This is one of the most popular types of business entity people forms to it avoid double taxation. It is taxed similarly to a partnership entity. But an S Corp. needs to be approved to be classified as such, it is also very common among auto dealers to choose this business structure as well.

LIMITED LIABILITY COMPANY (LLC)

This is the most common business structure among auto dealership businesses. It offers benefits for small businesses since it reduces the risk of losing all your personal assets in case you are faced with a lawsuit. It provides a clear separation between business and personal assets. You can also elect to be taxed as a corporation, which saves you money come tax time.

If you are unsure which specific business structure you should choose then, you can discuss it with an accountant. They will direct you in the best possible option for what your business goals are.

Here is a sample article of incorporation for an LLC entity

STATE OF ALABAMA:

COUNTY OF BALDWIN:

ARTICLES OF ORGANIZATION

OF

B&B AUTO Brokers LLC

The undersigned, acting as organizers of the B&B Auto Brokers LLC under the Alabama Limited Liability Company Act, adopt the following Articles of Organization for said Limited Liability Company.

Article I

Name of the Company

The name of the limited liability company is B&B Auto Brokers LLC (the "Company").

Article II

Period of Duration

The period of duration is ninety (90) years from the date of filing of these Articles of Organization with the Alabama Secretary of State, unless the Company is sooner dissolved.

Article III

Purpose of the Company

The Company is organized to engage in all legal and lawful purpose of used auto sales business.

Article IV

Registered Office and Agent

The Company's registered office is at address is 123 Main Court, Daphne, Alabama 36561; and the name and the address of the Company's initial registered agent is John Doe, 123 Main Court, Daphne, Alabama 36561

Article V

Members of the Organization

There is one (1) member, all of which are identified in the Exhibit A attached hereto and a part hereof. The initial capital contribution agreed to be made by both members are also listed on Exhibit A. The members have not agreed to make any additional contributions, but may agree to do so in the future upon the terms and conditions as set forth in the Operating Agreement.

Article VI

Additional Members

The members, as identified in the Company's Operating Agreement, reserve the right to admit additional members and determine the Capital Contributions of such Members. Notwithstanding the foregoing, the additional Members may not become managing unless and until selected to such position as provided in Article VII of the Company's Operating Agreement.

Article VII

Contribution upon Withdrawal of Members

The members shall have the right to continue the company upon the death, retirement, resignation, expulsion, bankruptcy or dissolution of a member or occurrence of any event which terminates the continued membership of a member in the Company (collectively, "Withdrawal"), as long as there is at least One remaining member, and the remaining member agree to continue the Company by unanimous written consent within 90 days after the Withdrawal of a Member, as set forth in the Operating Agreement of the Company.

Article VIII

Manager

The name and business address of the initial manager is:

John Doe

B&B Auto Brokers LLC

123 Main Court

Daphne, Alabama 36561

The manager may be removed and replaced by the Members as provided in the Operating Agreement.

IN WITNESS WHEREOF, the undersigned have caused these Articles of Organization to be executed this ……………. Day of ……………………….. 2010

_____

_____

        B&B Auto Brokers LLC

DATE

AN ALABAMA CORPORATION

BY: John Doe

ITS: Managing Member

This instrument prepared by:

Jane Doe

999 Super Ct

Daphne, Al 36561

EXHIBIT A

MEMBERS INTEREST   INTIAL CONTRIBUTION

John Doe   Future Services Rendered   100%

EIN NUMBER FROM IRS

EIN or Employer Identification number is essentially a social security or tax identification number but for your business. IRS and many other governmental agencies can identify your business via this unique 9 digit number.

Remember you will not need this number if you choose to be a sole proprietorship for your business.

It is simple to apply, either you can do it yourself or get your accountant to apply for you, but the process is simple, you fill out the form SS-4, which can be filed online, via Fax or via mail.

Here is a link to IRS website where you can download or fill out the form online.

https://www.irs.gov/businesses/small-businesses-self-employed/how-to-apply-for-an-ein

Form SS-4
(Rev. January 2010)
Department of the Treasury
Internal Revenue Service

Application for Employer Identification Number

(For use by employers, corporations, partnerships, trusts, estates, churches, government agencies, Indian tribal entities, certain individuals, and others.)

► See separate instructions for each line. ► Keep a copy for your records.

OMB No. 1545-0003

EIN

Type or print clearly.

1 Legal name of entity (or individual) for whom the EIN is being requested

2 Trade name of business (if different from name on line 1)

3 Executor, administrator, trustee, "care of" name

4a Mailing address (room, apt., suite no. and street, or P.O. box)

5a Street address (if different) (Do not enter a P.O. box)

4b City, state, and ZIP code (if foreign, see instructions)

5b City, state, and ZIP code (if foreign, see instructions)

6 County and state where principal business is located

7a Name of responsible party

7b SSN, ITIN, or EIN

8a Is this application for a limited liability company (LLC) (or a foreign equivalent)? ☐ Yes ☐ No

8b If 8a is "Yes," enter the number of LLC members ►

8c If 8a is "Yes," was the LLC organized in the United States? ☐ Yes ☐ No

9a Type of entity (check only one box). Caution. If 8a is "Yes," see the instructions for the correct box to check.
☐ Sole proprietor (SSN)
☐ Partnership
☐ Corporation (enter form number to be filed) ►
☐ Personal service corporation
☐ Church or church-controlled organization
☐ Other nonprofit organization (specify) ►
☐ Other (specify) ►
☐ Estate (SSN of decedent)
☐ Plan administrator (TIN)
☐ Trust (TIN of grantor)
☐ National Guard
☐ Farmers' cooperative
☐ REMIC
☐ State/local government
☐ Federal government/military
☐ Indian tribal governments/enterprises

Group Exemption Number (GEN) if any ►

9b If a corporation, name the state or foreign country (if applicable) where incorporated
State | Foreign country

10 Reason for applying (check only one box)
☐ Started new business (specify type) ►
☐ Hired employees (Check the box and see line 13.)
☐ Compliance with IRS withholding regulations
☐ Other (specify) ►
☐ Banking purpose (specify purpose) ►
☐ Changed type of organization (specify new type) ►
☐ Purchased going business
☐ Created a trust (specify type) ►
☐ Created a pension plan (specify type) ►

11 Date business started or acquired (month, day, year). See instructions.

12 Closing month of accounting year

13 Highest number of employees expected in the next 12 months (enter -0- if none). If no employees expected, skip line 14.
Agricultural | Household | Other

14 If you expect your employment tax liability to be $1,000 or less in a full calendar year and want to file Form 944 annually instead of Forms 941 quarterly, check here. (Your employment tax liability generally will be $1,000 or less if you expect to pay $4,000 or less in total wages.) If you do not check this box, you must file Form 941 for every quarter. ☐

15 First date wages or annuities were paid (month, day, year). Note. If applicant is a withholding agent, enter date income will first be paid to nonresident alien (month, day, year) ►

16 Check one box that best describes the principal activity of your business.
☐ Construction ☐ Rental & leasing ☐ Transportation & warehousing ☐ Health care & social assistance ☐ Wholesale-agent/broker
☐ Real estate ☐ Manufacturing ☐ Finance & insurance ☐ Accommodation & food service ☐ Wholesale-other ☐ Retail
☐ Other (specify) ►

17 Indicate principal line of merchandise sold, specific construction work done, products produced, or services provided.

18 Has the applicant entity shown on line 1 ever applied for and received an EIN? ☐ Yes ☐ No
If "Yes," write previous EIN here ►

Third Party Designee
Complete this section only if you want to authorize the named individual to receive the entity's EIN and answer questions about the completion of this form.
Designee's name | Designee's telephone number (include area code)
Address and ZIP code | Designee's fax number (include area code)

Under penalties of perjury, I declare that I have examined this application, and to the best of my knowledge and belief, it is true, correct, and complete.
Name and title (type or print clearly) ►

Applicant's telephone number (include area code)

Applicant's fax number (include area code)

OPENING A COMMERCIAL BANK ACCOUNT

This is one important step, but it can only be done after you have a fully executed article of incorporation which has been approved by the state, and you have an EIN number assigned by the IRS.

Once you have these two documents, you should be able to go to a bank and open your first commercial bank account.

But remember to check and understand various types of commercial checking account fees, you want to find a bank that offers free or almost free commercial checking account because some larger banks can charge you hundreds of dollars each month depending on how many transactions you do. Make sure to ask and shop around before you sign on the dotted line.

REQUIRED FORMS AND DOCUMENTS

1. Bill of Sale.
2. Trade-in Equity Disclosure Statements.
3. Odometer Disclosure Statements.
4. Test Drive Agreements.

5. Privacy Statements.
6. Notices of Liability Insurance Requirement.
7. Delivery and Acceptance Statements.
8. Used Car Appraisal Forms.(If there is a Trade-in)
9. Commission Vouchers.
10. Title application

You will also need some other supplies that are essential for a car dealership. Like this image, you see this on most every new or used cars,

Here is a site you can buy all your forms and supplies from at a reasonable price.

http://www.sidsavage.com/

Here is another site "IDEA" where you can download and print some of the required forms. It can be a great resource, but this site requires a membership fee.

http://autodealeredu.com/index.php/free-printable-forms

AUCTION HOUSES

Once you get your dealer's license, it is time to get registered as a buyer with at least one or two of the biggest auction houses in North America. There are many smaller auction houses around the country, but I only prefer to deal with these two.

1. Manheim
2. ADESA

Out of the two, Manheim is the biggest auction house. They have hundreds of location throughout the country, and I am pretty sure there is one within short driving distance from you.

Once registered, you can log on to their site and see all upcoming auctions and their run list for each auction. You will be able to see each car and all their condition reports and status along with something call MMR (Manheim Market Report) which is an estimated price based on previous sales of the same or similar type of vehicles.

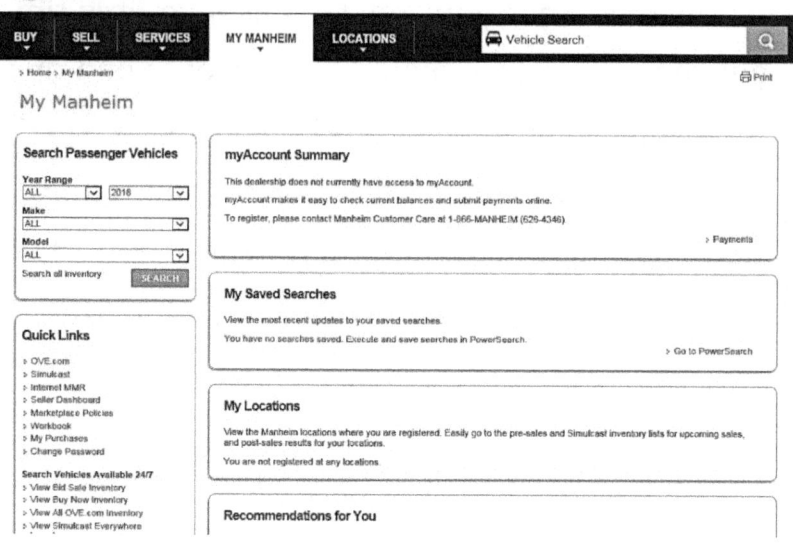

If you chose to, you can see every detail of a car right from your desktop and even proxy bid on them ahead of time or at the time of auction again right from home. It used to be where we had to go to the auction early in the morning, inspect each car we wanted to bid then when they were pulled up to the auction block, we would stand and bid on them. That is not the case anymore; you can do all that from home or office now.

But that doesn't mean you can't go anymore, yes many dealers especially the small dealers that buy cheaper cars, still go and look at each vehicle before bidding.

One thing to remember here, there are 4 types of cars each auction house sell

1. Green light cars
2. Yellow light cars
3. Red light cars
4. Blue Light cars

Green Light – "Ride and Drive": The green light signals that this vehicle is guaranteed under the conditions outlined in the Arbitration Guidelines section, except for specific disclosures or announcements made prior to the sale.

Green light cars are the ones that are sold as perfect condition cars, and the auction offers some degree of warranty on each of these vehicles. Say, you saw a car that is in great shape, the condition report scored it at 4 out of 5. You buy the car, and once it arrives, you noticed the transmission has issue, or there is a huge dent which was not mentioned on the CR(condition report), you can simple call the auction house and return it, they will even pay to transport it back to their facility and you will get a full refund.

Yellow Light – "Announcements": This light is an indication to the Buyer that the Auctioneer or Selling Representative has made announcements that qualify/clarify the condition or equipment and limit arbitration of this vehicle. This light can be used in conjunction with any other light.

On the yellow light cars, there are some issues, often these cars may be missing the actual title or some other paperwork, or there is an issue which prevented them from getting onto the green light status. It is best to review each vehicle that is under the yellow light to see what the actual issue is. Yellow does not necessarily mean they are lemons or bad cars.

Red Light – "As-Is": Vehicles selling under the red light will only qualify for arbitration under the rules outlined in the Arbitration Guidelines section. (As-Is dollar amount, model years, and mileage is subject to local auction policy). On the other hand cars with red light means they do have serious issues, like motor, transmission or they have a salvage title or other similar issues.

Anytime you are buying a car that is selling under the red light; you need to be extra careful.

Blue Light – "Title Attached/Title Unavailable/Title Absent": This light is used to announce that the title is not present at the time of the sale. For Auction rules regarding titles, please refer to the Title Arbitration Policy section. If "title attached/unavailable/absent" is not announced, a vehicle could be arbitrated for misrepresentation.

HOW TO GET STARTED ON A BUDGET

ACCORDING to the most reliable and reputable Manheim market report for 2015. "Autos have been a gem in an otherwise dull economy, with new unit sales in 2015 up 68 percent from 2009's trough. Auto loans outstanding have grown from $700 billion in 2011 to over $1.1 trillion today. NAAA-member auction sales rose 6.3 percent in 2015 to 9.3 million units, and volumes will continue to rise in 2016 and 2017.

Meanwhile, wholesale prices have been on an elevated progression for six years; increases in 2015 brought prices to near-record levels (just 1.2 percent short of 2011 high). With wholesale auto transactions taking place through numerous buying channels, technology tools emphasizing speed and efficiency are more critical than ever. New vehicle sales increased for an unprecedented sixth consecutive year, and the total, 17.5 million, was a record. Franchised dealers also recorded increased used vehicle sales for the sixth straight year, while a record 2.5 million certified pre-owned units were sold.

Dealers consigned 56.5 percent of all units sold at wholesale auctions in 2015. The average price of a used car in the United States in about $9,000. The used car market is flourishing as more and more people choose to save money by purchasing used cars instead of new vehicles."

I quoted the above numbers directly from their report, not anything I just made up. Here is a link that report, you can find on the web.

http://www.manheim.com/Market-report 2016

These are some truly fantastic numbers, and they are real numbers, not estimates. This number alone should motivate you to start your journey into the used car business. While you are going to need some capital to start a used car dealership; when you start small from home, you won't need as much money. In fact, starting a used car dealership from home has relatively low capital compared to other small scale businesses you could start. This makes it easier for you to get started in the business of selling used cars.

Let's estimate how much money you will need to get started from home.

(A gross estimate only)

All licensing fees	$750
Bond	$450
Insurance	$1850
Dealer Supplies	$500
Signage	$800
Total	$4,350

This will get you started without inventory, now let's assume you want to start out with just 1-2 cars, then you are looking at around $5,000-$8,000 each car. This will get you started.

But if you have access to more funds or capital, then you can start out with more cars, but to start small which I strongly suggest you do start out small and see how you like this line of business, you should go with 1-2 cars initially.

However, the demographic and psychographic aspects of a used car dealership are vast and can vary widely depending on the state you are planning to open your business. Some states are going to require more capital to start a used car dealership than others. In some states, you are likely to have more sales than others. This is why it is important to research the market in your state before choosing to open a used car dealership from your home.

But to argue my own point, I will say, regardless how many car dealers are around you, there will always be that need for reliable used cars, and I strongly suggest you start out with cars like Toyota Camry and other similar types of family cars and if you are in the southern regions, then trucks are always a big seller.

HOW TO GET FINANCING

IT DOESN'T take a lot of money to get started with a used car dealership. As you can tell by the table earlier for the regulations, you are going to need some money to get started based on license fees, insurance, and bonds. However, beyond this, the financing needed to start a car dealership from home is minimal since you'll likely be starting small with your inventory.

If you are going to need financing for your car dealership you want to start early. Finding the capital needed to start any business venture, no matter how small, can be a challenging prospect. In order to get capital from financial institutions or angel investors, you need to have a workable and promising business idea.

The first thing you need before looking for capital is a business plan. You likely already have one of these since you have probably already applied for your dealership license. If you have a sound business plan, then you will be able to easily convince investors to back your business. Without a sound business plan, investors won't take your seriously, and most banks won't extend a loan to you.

When it comes to getting financing for a used car dealership you have several options to look into, such as the following:

- Personal savings or sale of personal stocks if you don't need a large amount of money.

- Money from investors and/or business partners if you need a larger amount.

- Getting a loan from a bank if you have excellent credit.

- Applying for business grants and seed funding from donor organizations and angel investors by pitching your business idea.

- Getting soft loans from family or friends if you don't need a large amount to start.

- Lastly and the most common one is getting a "floor plan" from the auction houses.

If you already have funds saved up then you won't need any other help, but most do not have a large sum of cash saved up to start a business, I didn't.

The second option, as I mentioned is getting a partnership with someone who has access to money or finding a rich investor. But for this, you may need to show them (via a well-written business plan) how you plan to make money with this new business.

The third option is getting a loan from the bank. Another hard choice, for this you have to have excellent credit along with some asset and a great business plan where you can show the loan officer how you plan to be successful and repay their loan.

The fourth one is an option but not for everyone. This option requires a lot of creativity and people skills. If you have those, you can certainly give it a try.

The fifth option is easy. All you have to do is convince your friends and family to invest with you for either a small profit or some share of your business or just a soft loan which you will pay back within a specified time frame.

The last one is what most car dealers use. They apply and get a "floor plan" which is essentially a floating loan from the auction house like Manheim or ADESA. These plans are somewhat flexible; they may offer you 30-60 days with no interest, meaning as long as you pay back within that time frame, there is no interest on the loan.

Most mid to large size dealers use this plan to buy their inventory. But you will need good credit and financial records for this one to get approved.

In order to secure the financing you are often going to need all your legal paperwork in order. The business plan is a good place to start because it can act as a guidebook for what legal paperwork you need to acquire. Let's look at some of the legal aspects of starting a used car dealership.

LEGAL REQUIREMENTS

For a used car dealership in the United States there isn't a huge list of required legal documents, not much more than you would have for a typical business. Yet you still want to have these in order so your business can run smoothly without issues. Some of the basic legal documents that you should get in order include the following:

- ✓ Insurance
- ✓ Tax Payer's ID
- ✓ Fire Inspection Certificate
- ✓ Certificate of Incorporation
- ✓ Business License
- ✓ Business Plan
- ✓ Non-disclosure Agreement
- ✓ Employment Agreement
- ✓ Employee's Handbook

- ✓ Operating Agreement if you are going to file as an LLC

- ✓ Facility Permit / License

- ✓ Franchise or Trademark License (If applicable)

- ✓ Contract Documents for customers, shipping partners, etc.

- ✓ Online Terms of Use (If you have an online store or website)

- ✓ Online Privacy Policy (If you have an online store or website

USED CAR RULE

The Used Car Rule was once known as the Used Motor Vehicle Trade Regulation Rule. It has been in effect since 1985. This rule requires car dealers to display a window sticker known as the Buyers Guide on all used cars they offer for sale.

The Buyers Guide discloses whether a warranty is offered and if so what the terms and conditions are such as the duration of coverage, the percentage of total repair costs the dealer pays and which vehicle systems are covered by the warranty. If you are in a state that doesn't allow used cars to be sold "as is" or without warranties, then you need to display an alternative Buyers Guide. Used car sellers need to comply with the Used Car Rule. Let's take a look at what you need to know.

The Used Car Rule is established by the Federal Trade Commission (FTC). Anyone who sells or offers for sale more than five used vehicles within a twelve month period have to comply with this rule. The only ones exempt from this rule are banks and financial institutions, businesses that sell vehicles to employees and lessors who sell a leased vehicle to a lessee.

The Used Car Rule applies in all states except Wisconsin and Maine. These two states are exempt because they have regulations that require used car dealers to post disclosures. The rules also apply to the territories of the District of Columbia, Puerto Rico, Guam, the US Virgin Islands and American Samoa.

A Buyers Guide needs to be posted before a vehicle is displayed for sale or a customer is allowed to inspect it, even if the car isn't entirely ready for delivery. A Buyers Guide is also required on any used vehicles being sold through consignment, power of attorney or other agreement. At a public auction, the dealer and Auction Company need to follow the rule. However, if an auction is closed to consumers, then the rule doesn't apply.

Whether titled or not, any vehicle that is driven for any purpose other than moving or test driving is viewed as a used vehicle. This includes light-duty vans/trucks, demonstrators, and program cars that fit in the following categories:

- A gross vehicle weight rating (GVWR) of 8,500 pounds or less.
- A curb weight of 6,000 pounds or less.
- A frontal area 46 square feet or lower.

The exceptions to the rule are the following:

- Motorcycles.

➢ Vehicles sold for scrap or parts if the title documents are submitted to the appropriate state authority and a salvage certification is obtained.

➢ Agricultural equipment.

THE BUYERS GUIDE

BUYERS GUIDE

IMPORTANT. Spoken promises are difficult to enforce. Ask the dealer to put all promises in writing. Keep this form.

VEHICLE MAKE   MODEL   YEAR   VIN NUMBER

DEALER STOCK NUMBER (optional)

WARRANTIES FOR THIS VEHICLE:

☐ **AS IS - NO WARRANTY**

YOU WILL PAY ALL COSTS FOR ANY REPAIRS. The dealer assumes no responsibility for any repairs regardless of any oral statements about the vehicle

☐ **WARRANTY**

☐ FULL ☐ LIMITED WARRANTY. The dealer will pay ____ % of the labor and ____ % of the parts for the covered systems that fail during the warranty period. Ask the dealer for a copy of the warranty document for a full explanation of warranty coverage, exclusions, and the dealer's repair obligations. Under state law, "implied warranties" may give you even more rights.

SYSTEMS COVERED: DURATION:

☐ SERVICE CONTRACT: A service contract is available at an extra charge on this vehicle. Ask for details as to coverage, deductible, price, and exclusions. If you buy a service contract within 90 days of the time of sale, state law "implied warranties" may give you additional rights.

☐ PRE PURCHASE INSPECTION. ASK THE DEALER IF YOU MAY HAVE THIS VEHICLE INSPECTED BY YOUR MECHANIC EITHER ON OR OFF THE LOT.

SEE THE BACK OF THIS FORM for important additional information, including a list of some major defects that may occur in used motor vehicles.

The Buyers Guide is a disclosure document that provides consumers with purchasing and warranty information. The Buyers Guide is designed to tell the consumer the following:

- ❖ The car's major mechanical and electrical systems, along with the major problems a consumer should be aware of for the vehicle.
- ❖ If the vehicle is being sold "as is" or with a warranty.
- ❖ If a vehicle is under warranty, what percentage of repair costs the dealer pays.
- ❖ That oral promises are difficult to enforce.
- ❖ That all promises should be received in writing.
- ❖ That you should have an independent mechanic inspect the car before buying.
- ❖ To get a vehicle history report.
- ❖ To get information on how to check for safety recalls and other related topics.
- ❖ To get a Spanish Buyers Guide if the sale is made in Spanish.

- To retain the Buyers Guide as a reference after the sale.

The Buyers Guide needs to be displayed in a prominent and conspicuous location on or in the vehicle once it is available for sale. This means it needs to be in plain view with both sides visible. The guide can be hung from the rear-view mirror inside the car or on a side-view mirror outside the car.

It can also be placed under the windshield wiper or attached to a side window. You cannot plan a Buyer's Guide in a glove compartment, trunk or under the seat since they aren't in plain sight. A Buyers Guide can be removed for a test drive but must be replaced as soon as the test drive is completed.

Let's consider all the areas of a Buyer's Guide and what information is should include.

VEHICLE INFORMATION

This is the top portion of the guide and should include the vehicle make, model, model year and vehicle identification number (VIN). If you want, you can also include the dealer stock number.

DEALER INFORMATION

On the back of the guide, you should have the name and address of your dealership. You should also fill in the name (or position) and telephone number of the person the consumer should contact if there are complaints.

You can choose to preprint your guide with this information or use a rubber stamp to place the information on the guide before displaying.

OPTIONAL SIGNATURE LINE

It is your option to include a signature line on the Guide that you can ask the buyer to sign in order to acknowledge that they received the Guide. If you are going to include a signature line, then you will need a nearby disclosure that says: "I hereby acknowledge receipt of the Buyers Guide at the closing of this sale."

You can preprint this on the form, and it needs to appear in the space provided for the name of the individual they contact if they have a complaint about the sale.

VEHICLE WARRANTY

There are two versions of the Buyers Guide: One is an "As Is - No Dealer Warranty" and the other is an "Implied Warranties Only." Let's consider the difference between these two.

If a state allows it you can have an "As Is - No Dealer Warranty," which allows you to not offer a warranty both implied, expressed and written. For this, you need to use the "As Is" version of the Buyers Guide and check the box next to the heading "As Is - No Dealer Warranty."

The other options are "Implied Warranties Only." This is often found in states that limit or prohibit the elimination of implied warranties. Again you need to use the "Implied Warranties Only" version of the Buyers Guide and check the box next to the heading for "Implied Warranties Only" if you aren't going to offer a written warranty.

If you are going to offer an express warranty with your vehicles, then you need to check the box next to the heading "Warranty" and fill in the section of the guide designed for this. In this section, you need to disclose any warranties that are required by law in your state. You can learn about your states warranty requirements through the state Attorney General.

FULL OR LIMITED WARRANTY

In order for a warranty to be considered full it needs to include the following:

- Warranty service needs to be provided to anyone who owns a vehicle under the warranty period.

- The warranty service needs to be free of charge if necessary, even for removing and reinstalling systems covered by the warranty.

- The consumer has the right to choose a replacement or a refund if the vehicle isn't able to be repaired after a reasonable number of tries.

- The consumer doesn't have to do anything to receive service, expect to give notice of needed service. After notice, service must be rendered unless the warrantor can demonstrate that the consumer was reasonable required to give additional notice.

> The length of an implied warranty can't be limited in any way.

A warranty is considered limited if any of these conditions can't be applied to the warranty.

On the Buyers Guide, you'll also be required to fill in the percentage of parts and labor costs that you cover under warranty. If there is a deductible to repairs made under warranty, then place an asterisk next to the number and explain the deductible under the "systems covered/duration" section of the Buyers Guide.

There is a column available for you to list the systems covered and another list to show the length of the warranty for each system. If the left column you need to specify each system that you cover under warranty.

The Used Car Rule prohibits you from using shorthand phrases since they aren't clear what specific components are included. If the right-hand column, you need to list the length of warranty for each system. If all systems are covered for the same length of time, then you only have to state the duration once.

If you happen to have a vehicle that is still under the manufacturer's warranty, then you can disclose this to the consumer by checking the box, "Manufacturer's Warranty Still Applies." This is found in the Non-Dealer Warranties for the vehicle section of the Buyers Guide. You cannot check this box if the consumer needs to pay for coverage under the manufacturer's warranty. This type of coverage is considered a service contract.

On the other hand, you can still check the box if you pay for coverage from the manufacturer and the consumer won't need to pay anything more than the cost of the vehicle to get covered. If you are going to provide a warranty in addition to the unexpired manufacturer's warranty, then you need to explain the terms of your warranty on the Buyers Guide.

Should you negotiate for changes to the warranty with the consumer, the changes need to be reflected in the Buyers Guide. You need to cross out the original disclosure and write in the new disclosure. If you are changing from an "as is" vehicle to one with a warranty, then you must fill out the warranty section in full for the Buyers Guide to be properly completed.

Lastly, if you offer a service contract for repairs then you check the box next to "Service Contract." If the state you are in regulates service contracts as a "business of insurance" then you don't have to check the box. You state Attorney General or State Insurance Commissioner can help you find out if your state regulates service contracts as insurance.

WHAT YOU HAVE TO PROVIDE AT THE SALE

At the time of sale you need to provide the original Buyers Guide or a copy to the consumer. All final changes need to be reflected in the Buyers Guide. If you have a signature line, make sure the consumer signs the Guide once it reflects all changes.

Under FTC Rules and the Magnuson-Moss Warranty Act, you must follow the "Warranty Disclosure Rule" if you are offering a written warranty or if the manufacturer's warranty still applies. This Rule contains provisions that establish consumer rights when it comes to written warranties.

The Rule prohibits you from eliminating implied warranties when giving a written warranty. It does this by requiring that you disclose certain information regarding the coverage of your warranty and the consumers' rights under your state's law. This information needs to be in a single document that is clear and easy to read.

The warranty information provided in the Buyers Guide isn't sufficient to meet the requirements of the Warranty Disclosure Rule. Your written warranty and the Buyers Guide are required to be two separate documents. In addition, the FTCs Rule on Pre-Sale Availability of Written Warranty Terms requires you to display a written warranty in close proximity to the vehicle or make them available to consumers on request.

Lastly, there is the option of the split cost warranties. These are where the dealer pays less than 100% of the cost for a warranty repair. This is known as a 50/50 warranty, where the dealer pays 50% of the cost for a covered repair and the consumers pay the other 50%. There are other types of split cost warranties where the consumer pays a deductible amount, and the dealer pays the remaining costs.

If you are going to offer one of these split cost warranties then you need to include the following disclosure in your warranty document:

➢ The percentage of the total cost you will pay.

➢ The percentage of the total cost the consumer must pay.

➢ How the total cost of the repair will be determined.

If you require consumers to pay a deductible, then your warranty document needs to disclose the deductible amount and the details of when and under what circumstances the deductible has to be paid.

If you are offering a split cost warranty, then you can require the consumer to return to the dealer for warranty repairs. If you are going to include this restriction, then you should provide an estimate of the total repair cost before starting work. This allows the consumer to determine whether or not they want to approve the repair work or have it done elsewhere.

GETTING COPIES OF THE BUYERS GUIDE

You can go to the FTCs Business Center online and download the Buyers Guide, or you can get them from business-form companies or trade associations. You can also make them yourself on the computer as long as you make sure the wording, type style, type sizes and format follow those specified in the Used Car Rule.

You can't place any other type of wording or symbols on the Buyers Guide. The Buyers Guide must be in black ink on white papers to a size of 11" x 7 1/4". You can't modify these requirements in any way unless you are using colored ink to fill in the blank spaces.

If you don't comply with these rules, then you can be subject to penalties up to $40,000 under FTC enforcement actions. A lot of states have their own laws and regulations similar to the Used Car Rule. Some states also incorporate the Used Car Rule into their state laws. This is why it is important to check with you local legal representative to find out what you need to do to be in compliance.

DEVELOPING YOUR INVENTORY

THE only way to be successful as a used car dealer is to have a steady supply of good quality used cars. One of the first steps in your business strategy should be to explore the best options for finding a way of getting various types of used cars.

If you have a good network of people, you can easily find people who want to sell their used cars. Other options are to place adverts on a variety of advertising platforms in order to tell people you are available to buy used cars. The internet is one of the busiest places to buy and sell used cars, so you should definitely include it in your plans to purchase cars and potentially to sell cars as well.

Even if you plan to sell cars only from your home or from a small brick and mortar location, you can still set up on online used car dealership. It doesn't cost much to set up an online store. You just need some good logistics. Also when you open an online car dealership, you won't restrict yourself to the target market of your location, but rather an entire online community.

At one-time vehicle sourcing wasn't that difficult. However, with today's conditions; sourcing the right mix of used vehicles for your dealership is becoming more difficult. Floor plan sources are more restrictive, and consumer spending has down periods.

A part of establishing good inventory means planning for reduced funding, fewer vehicle sales, and fewer trade-ins. One way to do this is to look beyond the standard car sales and trade-ins and to find other cost-effective ways to source used cars.

Before we consider sources of used cars it is important to remind yourself that you need to have the right mix of used vehicle inventory. You want to choose as your core, vehicles that are proven winners for used car dealership sales.

These are the vehicles that sell for more than the average price. You can find a number of inventory systems on the market to help you identify the best cars, or you can choose to keep track of your sales and determine what vehicles sell the best for the highest price in your area.

Another important thing to consider is your remarketing strategy. If you don't have the tactics necessary to create demand, then your vehicles will just sit on the lot and cost you money. A good remarketing strategy is one that considers a vehicle's past sales performance and aging history along with current market demands and residual value.

Used vehicles have a high degree of ambiguity which means you need to create demand for this unique commodity.

After you've found the best vehicles for your inventory and developed a remarketing strategy, you want to first consider your own database as a cost-effective source for inventory. Look at customers who have previously purchased a desirable vehicle from you within the last five years.

Also, consider your service department and look at the vehicles that are coming in with positive equity. Contact both of these customers to offer trade-ins on their vehicles; it will get your both additional sales and also the used vehicle inventory you need.

Another option is inter-group trading. If your dealership is a part of a multi-store group, then you can communicate to determine individual vehicle needs and transfer inventory as needed. This will reduce acquisition costs and reduce any wholesale losses.

Yet another option is to look at lost appraisals. Compile a list of completed appraisals within the last 30 days for all needed make/models. This will give you a targeted list of potential customers you can bring back into the sales cycle.

For me, the best sourcing is usually the auctions, mostly either Manheim or ADESA and sometimes both. I only buy Green light cars so I know they are in good condition and I can sell them without any worry.

As I mentioned before, if you are just starting out and on a tight budget, you should start out with something that sells fast. Now there are not just one or two cars that are hot seller everywhere. For example, in the up north most Subaru cars are very popular because of their all-wheel drive option which is easier to handle in the snow. In the Deep South, pickup trucks are very popular. But does that mean you only need to carry those? Not really, carry that sells everywhere regardless where you are and carry something that will sell faster than others.

That is the very reason I brought the example of 5-7-year-old Toyota Camry or Corolla. These type of cars are well known for their durability and frugality. If you buy one that has no major issue, if you price them right, you should have no problem selling that vehicle in just a week.

Provided you priced it right, took great pictures and advertised it in places where people look for cars in your area. Also when you are starting out, try to stay away from carrying colors like Red or Green, try to stay with more neutral colors while remembering that Black cars usually sell well.

Once you start to grow, you should then start to carry a few varieties and not all just Toyota sedans. Remember to be a successful dealer; you have to carry a few varieties even when you know some of those cars or trucks won't move fast.

No matter where you get your used vehicle inventory, you want to choose a buy and sell strategy that works for getting core vehicles and remarketing them to sell fast. This is key to proper inventory management and will help give you a competitive edge that leads to consistent profits. Along these lines let's look at how to sell your cars for the maximum profit.

HOW TO SELL CARS

KEY to keeping your business in operation is to make sure you do everything you can to be an honest used car dealer. By following the regulations for your state as we've already discussed, you will have a good, trustworthy image that will help you stand out from other used car competitors in your area.

Another way is to go above customer expectations with superior service and automobile repairs in order to improve your overall business image. All of this will impact your business success. Let's look at some ways you can improve your business and help sell used cars for maximum profit.

As we've discussed earlier in sourcing your inventory, you should look at used car auctions to increase your inventory. If you aren't experienced yet in getting cars, then bring along an expert to help you distinguish lemons and reliable cars that will sell on your lot. When considering vehicles do a rough estimate to determine how much labor is needed along with any repair cost on a car that may not be in excellent running condition. This estimate; along with information on make, model and year will help you to determine which vehicles will make you a decent profit when selling.

Never bid more than you feel a vehicle is worth if it requires too many repairs to turn a decent profit. After paying for your used cars at the auction, obtain the necessary paperwork and get prepared to turn the vehicle over for sale on your lot.

Once the vehicles arrive on your lot; inspect, repair and clean them, so they are ready to be sold. Unless you can do it yourself, you should hire a licensed mechanic to repair any vehicles. Make sure you document all repairs made. You may also want to source out to a professional auto detailer in order to clean the interior and exterior of used vehicles, so they are presentable to potential customers.

It is also important to maintain a good appearance for your car lot and showroom. Sweep regularly to keep down debris. Power was the exterior buildings and signs. Keep the offices clean and desks organized. Park, all your vehicles with equal space between them for an orderly appearance. At the same time make sure there is enough room between each vehicle to open the doors fully.

Make sure you offer a warranty on all vehicles you've serviced and repaired. Many people don't trust a used car dealer that offers a vehicle "as is." You can convince many customers to buy, simply by offering a sixty or ninety-day warranty.

It goes without saying, that a lot of customers are more likely to buy when you greet them and engage them in friendly conversation. If you are going to hire staff, make sure your assistants and salespeople are good at talking with customers and answer telephones. When you focus on customer needs, you'll do better in the sales area.

For each used vehicle on your lot make sure you calculate the bottom dollar. This is a figure that represents the absolute minimum you can sell a car for without losing profits. From this amount, add five to ten percent markup for dealer cost. When negotiating with potential customers keep this amount in mind. Also, make sure you assign trade-in value to vehicles that customers are potentially going to trade-in at your dealership. You can find these figures through the Kelley Blue Book or National Automotive Dealer Association.

The most important part of running a used car dealership is customer service. Offer free vehicle identification number reports or background checks from CARFAX.com or AutoCheck.com. Once you sell a car, don't end your customer service. Follow up with customers through direct mail or telephone calls in order to thank them and find out how things are going.

This can lead to repeat business for your dealership. In order to keep everything ordered and efficient it is important to have a good dealer software. Let's look at how you can find the right software for your used car dealership.

HOW MUCH CAN YOU MAKE

WHEN it comes to selling used cars, there's no definite number that you can set as to how much you will make. Selling used cars is very much based on the market and how well you can sell your vehicles and other services. If you are simply looking to make some extra money on the side by selling a few cars from home, then this may not be a problem for you.

However, if you plan on selling used cars as a primary means of income, then you'll want to look a little closer at just how much you can make selling used cars. The best way to do this is to consider how much a professional car salesperson can make at a big name dealer to get a ballpark figure of what you may make as a used car dealer.

First, you want to consider the fact that sometimes you'll have to lose money to make money. This can be especially true when selling used cars from home where you may not have a lot of room for inventory. Even on a larger professional lot, they need to move cars off to make room for others. This may mean taking a thousand dollar loss of some vehicles that aren't moving quickly enough.

So there may be times when you have to undersell that one vehicle just to make room for a vehicle you are able to sell for a higher price. This will have an overall impact on how much money you make.

Second, you need to keep in mind how front-end losses can be offset by your back-end profits. We'll discuss these aspects of finances in a moment. A happy customer who pays more for a vehicle will return for other services while a dissatisfied customer who gets a great deal will never return to make up for the lost cost of a vehicle.

The bottom line is that when you sell used cars from home, you stand a better chance of making a profit than working for a professional dealer. All of the profit you make goes straight to you and running your business. So as long as you keep your operating costs in mind and budget well, you can end up making a decent amount from your used car business. Let's consider how you can sell vehicles part time from home and make a nice profit.

FRONT END VS BACK END COMMISSIONS

One of the things you need to know when it comes to profits in used car sales is knowing the difference between front-end sales and back-end sales. Let's start by discussing front end sales.

When you sell a vehicle, the front end sale is the first sale. Basically, it is the vehicle the customer is buying. It is also the product with the lowest price. Think of it as an introductory offer. Now let's consider back end sales.

Back-end sales are often where used car dealers make the most money. This is because you offer people other items once they've already bought a vehicle from you. The customer now trusts you and is willing to spend more money with you. You will also be offering new products that will enhance the vehicle your customer has already purchased.

Back-end products you offer need to be related to the vehicle you are selling. The better your back end product offerings, the more trust and confidence you'll be increasing with your customer. You can sell as much as possible and earn a lot of additional profits. This goes along with learning how to grow your business

MAKE MONEY BY FINANCING

There are two ways you can make money while financing a vehicle for your customers. You have seen many local dealers with a sign "Buy Here Pay Here." Most of these dealers finance a vehicle by themselves; there is no bank or other financial institutions involved.

This is how it works, say you bought a car for $1800, then you spent $550 to fix whatever was wrong with it, then you put it for sale in your lot for $3599. You can sell this vehicle two ways if someone pays you the whole amount for it or you can finance part of this asking price. Most used car dealers try to get as much of their cost of the vehicle as down payment.

So in this case, if a customer wants you to finance this vehicle you can ask for $1500-$2000 down and rest you can finance for around six months to a year for 18-25% interest rate. Yes! It is high-interest rate but think about the risk involved in it. What if the customer stops making payment?

If you would have to track them down, hire a repo man and get the vehicle repossessed from them, bring it in, fix whatever is wrong with it, then resale it again. I personally do not recommend you try this route. But I know many small dealers love this business model.

My theory is to carry better cars this way you attract better customers who either can bring their own financing, or you can help them find a suitable financing option and make some money along the way. How may you ask?

Well, here is the fun part, if you carry late model cars, you can sign up with few local and big banks and credit unions as a vendor and once you find a buyer, you can submit deals to these banks via your dealer software (will discuss this next) and directly upload a credit app to their server and one of the loan specialists will reply back with a rate and terms, which in turn you take it to your customer and see if they agree.

If you ever went into large car dealers, I am sure you have seen how they operate. The sales person ask you to fill up a credit app, which they take it to the finance manager and a few minutes later they come back with 2-3 offers, if you put this much down, you get this rate and so on and so forth. See the best part is most banks offer you 1-2 percent cash back up front on most of these deals. Sounds confusing?

Okay, say a bank offered one of your customer 7% APR for 60 months on a 30K loan. If your customer agrees to the terms and signs up for that deal, the bank will send you 1% of the total loan value in 30 days. Which is $300. Not bad huh? But remember these negotiations are done beforehand with each lender, so you will know ahead of time which bank is offering what.

HOW TO SELL USED CARS PART TIME FROM HOME

IF YOU want to start a small business that you can do on a small budget then selling used cars from home is certainly a good option. This is an even better option if you have a good network of people who want to sell their used cars to you.

Once you have used cars in place, all you really need to do is get it out to the public that you have used cars for sale. The best way to do this is through the internet and a website. There are plenty of platforms on the internet that allow you to advertise your used cars for free.

Depending on the state you live in, you might also be allowed to park the vehicles in your front yard and place a sign on them. However, in order to really make a profit selling used cars you have to be ready to take on many roles at once and do the majority of the work yourself. This includes managing, accounting, car washing, servicing, etc.

When you do this, it can be relatively easy to make a $500 to $1500 profit per car you sell. Let's look at how you can do this.

If you don't get your dealer's license, you'll have to get most of your used cars from the classifieds. This can be an okay option but will require a lot of work on your part since you'll have to keep your eyes on multiple local sources.

However, with a dealer's license, you will have a simpler option of going to dealer auctions and getting a wide range of choices. The key is to look for cheap local cars that you can sell for profit or those that you can recondition easily and sell for a higher price.

Again the most important thing is to remember that customers like dealing with people and not dealers. If you are a people person who sells a mechanically sound car at a good deal, then the word is going to spread, and you'll be able to get both repeat business and word of mouth customers.

However, as I said before, if you really want to make a profit then you need to run the entire operation yourself. This means no office and no employees. You'll have to do all the searching for a car, recondition it yourself and do all the sales work; but you'll be able to keep all the profits.

One option you have when it comes to selling used cars is to use eBay. This allows you to sell used cars as a side business while still maintaining a full-time job if this is something you want to do. It can also be a good option for those who simply want a full time stay at home job.

On the weekends you need to go out and find cars to buy, but then you can save time and money by posting the car on eBay. The buyer will search the listing and come pick it up once they've won the auction. Nothing can be easier and take all the time and effort out of dealing with people coming to your home to buy a vehicle.

Another option for the at home used car dealer is to consider auto brokering. This is where you can arrange for the buying and selling of used cars for a fee or profit. This will require more of a selling personality than the eBay option, but will also pay you more and provide more opportunity for repeat business.

Obviously, the cheapest and lowest risk option is to simply start out part time with just a few cars each month. Buy a car, register it in your name, recondition it yourself and then the part is somewhere locally or advertise in a classified or on eBay. Once the car sells, you will have a profit and money to buy your next car to sell.

Selling just one car a week or two cars a month can easily get you a $1000 profit or more. There isn't much too it and how much you make really depends on how much you want to put into the buying and selling process. By keeping your operating costs low, you won't have any trouble making a profit.

However, as we've already discussed before; you are going to have to adhere to state limits that may make it a little harder to operate an at home used car dealership and make a profit. Most states have a limit before you need to get a dealer's license while other states require everyone who sells a car to get a license. If you stay under the limit, then you can certainly keep your costs down by avoiding all the regulations that come with getting a dealer's license.

If you are going to sell beyond the state limit, then you'll need to decide whether or not it is worth the cost of getting a dealer's license and starting a used car dealership. As you've seen before there are a lot of costs and operating fees that go into starting a used car dealership.

As a result, most people choose to simply limit a number of cars they sell in a year and have a little extra cash on hand that they can use for a nice vacation. You will certainly have to sit down and consider the costs of starting a used car dealership versus potential profits in order to determine what option is right for you. Let's summarize the pros and cons of selling from home to help make your decision a little easier.

PROS

- ❖ You have the option of starting small without a dealer's license.

- ❖ You have the option of starting slow without a lot of financial risks.

- ❖ You can take your time to inspect a car.

- ❖ You can easily expand your business into retailing or wholesaling as you get more experienced with selling used cars.

- ❖ You can start and stop the used car business anytime you want.

CONS

- ❖ You are limited to buying cars from individuals, which requires a lot of time and energy since only licensed dealers are allowed to go to the dealer only auctions.

- ❖ Registering vehicles in your name can impact your profits since you are going to have to pay sales tax on the vehicles until you sell them.

- ❖ You are limited by the state as to the number of cars you can buy and sell.

When it comes to buying and selling from home there are ten things you need to keep in mind in order to have a profit work from home business:

1. Inspect each car and take your time to do it thoroughly. Don't allow your emotions to take over during the process.

2. Start out your business with a single type of car and learn everything you need about it.

3. Specialize your business as you grow and focus on just one or two makes of cars. Stick with vehicles that have the best resale value.

4. Avoid illegal practices such as curb stoning.

5. Keep your work from home business as a single person operation. This allows you to keep all the profits yourself with only having to re-invest the profits into the business.

6. Don't buy any project cars. These will only be a waste of your time and money.

7. Spend as little as you can on repairs and if you need to do some, make sure you can do as much as possible on your own.

8. Make sure the cars you sell are mechanically sound, clean and pleasant looking. Would you drive the cars yourself?

9. If possible make sure you sell all cars as-is with no warranty.

10. Don't finance anything until you get a lot. Accept only cash, cashier's check or money orders.

CHOOSING THE BEST DEALER SOFTWARE

A DEALER management software is a tool a program that can pretty much runs your dealership. It has modules that can be customized to fit your exact needs.

A good dealer software can:

- Track and keep up with your inventory
- Can run your service and repair business
- Can help you finance a vehicle
- Can store all your customer and employee information
- Employee time tracking
- Payroll
- and much more

But when you are just starting out, you will not need this; you will see the need to have such software. But when you do need it, here are a few things to remember before you decide on one.

When it comes to dealer software, you want something that does everything you need while also delivering the ROI you want. As a used auto dealer you know about making complex and big decisions. It is important to keep in mind that your customers are also wrestling with a big purchase decision. Answer their questions and wait for them to weight the pros and cons of a big decision.

You can also help guide them through the process if they've never been through it before. One way you can make the process easier for everyone is to get a good dealer software that meets your needs and helps solve your problems. Let's look at how you can choose the right dealer software for your business.

First, if you are going to hire employees or work with other individuals, you want to make sure everyone is invested in your new software. No matter what software solution you choose, it won't do any good if people don't actually use it.

You also don't want to pay out a lot of money for something that isn't going to be used. You won't have to worry about this much if you are selling from your home, but if you are going to have even one employee you want to get input from all key players in your business. Find out what problems exist and what they need the new software to do. From here you can choose software that meets these needs.

This is where a lot of larger auto dealers make a mistake; they don't focus on the salespeople when choosing software. You are going to rely on your software most when making a sale. So focus on this aspect of your software first, but don't neglect other areas as well.

Second, you want to choose a system that meets your needs by actually knowing what your needs are. Make sure yourself and anyone you work with agree on what the ideal software solution is. Are you looking to improve existing processes or are there gaps that need to be filled?

What will a software offer your business and will it work with your existing systems? It is important to write down the features and capabilities that you absolutely need in software and have this information on hand when researching dealer software. Make sure you choose a software that can meet as many needs as possible.

Dealer software can be a major investment. Therefore, the third area to consider is the value versus the price. When you choose the right dealer software, you'll be able to have a big return on your investment.

So when setting a budget for your dealer software, it is important to remember that setting the budget slightly higher can often get you the additional functioning you need. However, you also want to keep in mind the cost of integration, overages and user licenses. All of these fees will add up, but some of them you can avoid by reading the small print.

Remember that you're not the only one looking for dealer software. Talk to other dealerships or employees who have used other systems in the past. Determine software that they would recommend and others that they would avoid. Getting the insight from others can go a long way to reducing your options.

If you don't have anyone locally, you can ask, then consider going to online forums to getting reviews of dealer software.

It is also a good idea to try out software demos. This can be a great way to determine whether or not a software is going to meet your needs. During the demo be sure to ask questions and make sure you get all the answers you need and check all of your requirements.

Rather than simply getting a yes or no answer; work to find out the how since a yes answer may be different based on the software you are testing. As you demo software you will likely think of follow up questions, so don't be afraid to try a demo more than once. You can also ask a vendor to record the demo so you can refer to it later when making your final selection.

Lastly, once you've picked your top dealer software choices, you are at the step to make a final decision. Make sure you don't rush this decision. This is the time to carefully consider all your options and get the opinion of everyone that is going to be involved. Get the input of all key players and look over your notes from all the demos based on features, capabilities, and pricing.

Buying the right software for your used dealership takes time and effort, but you want to make sure you find the right software that provides you with what you need and delivers the ROI you want. All of this information may seem overwhelming and may make you a little apprehensive about getting into the used car business.

Here is a link all top dealer management software and their details, take a look, it is hard to recommend one specific brand of software since they vary so widely based the size of your business and what other additional services you sell along with cars.

But this a helpful site to get a clear idea on what and how the various software differs from one another. I personally have used Dealer Track for many years now; I am used to it, I love it, but that doesn't mean all the others are not good.

http://www.capterra.com/auto-dealer-software/

HOW TO GROW YOUR USED CAR DEALERSHIP

THE traditional way of selling a car is still popular today. This means buying a car at an auction or through other means if you don't have a dealer's license and then selling it through traditional advertising methods. However, there are a few things you can do to generate greater profits when selling cars from home.

First, consider selling vehicles through online auctions. This will give you access to more potential customers that traditional advertising methods. Most vehicle placed on online auction sites such as eBay will generate potential buyers from across the United States. Most vehicles posted online will sell within seven days or less.

Another option is to consider the revenue of buy here/pay here. Some used car dealers than to buy economical cars that are about $500 to $2000 wholesale. They then collect down payments from a customer that is near or equal to the cost of the vehicle and then get weekly payments until the car is paid in full. This can often give you a 100 to 200 percent return on investment.

Another way to generate quick profits is to consider wholesale vehicles. With this option, you are buying vehicles from one dealership or auction and then selling them within a few days to another. Since you are only holding vehicles for a few days, you will get steady process through a wholesale market.

As local customers get to know you for selling quality vehicles you may also get requests for specific vehicles. If this happens, you need to look for the make and model a customer wants and then deliver it to them. This it basically the same as having a guaranteed sale and makes the selling process easier for you.

You can also offer the option of buying customer vehicles or selling their vehicles for them. This can be an easy way to make a little extra money on the side. Offer to promote other vehicles for a small fee or take a commission on selling vehicles for someone else.

Lastly, you could consider offering classic cars or specialty cars. You can choose to purchase a classic vehicle that is ready to sell or one that only needs moderate work to be restored to selling condition. This can be a great way to expand your business and sell for a good profit.

It is nice that you can start a used car dealership without needing a lot of money and still make a profit. As long as you make yourself trustworthy and dependable to customers, you will be able to make a good profit.

Starting a used car dealership will be interesting and a good side business that provides rewards. Through diligent marketing strategies and good business functioning, you will be able to have a successful work from home business. So now you'll be prepared to get your work from home business off the ground and have some good success.

5 RAPID FIRE Q&A

HERE are few very common questions I get asked often:

How to bring cars from Auction to your lot?

If you are buying just one or two cars, and want to save money, you can take a friend or two and drive the cars back with you. But My recommendation is to contact your auction help desk and ask them to locate you a hauler.

Typically if your auction is within 300 miles from your lot, each car should cost you around $250-$275 to transport, but more cars you bring cheaper it gets.

How can I get the cars ready for sale?

Once your car is delivered, you have to do a thorough inspection to make sure the condition matches the CR report that you saw on the auction site online.

Also that there is no other mechanical or other hidden damages on the car. Once you are satisfied, get the car cleaned and detailed. Then put all necessary tags and stickers, along with your selling price (if you choose to do so), and park the car so potential buyers can see it from the road.

How to Price your Cars?

Say you just bought a 2013 Nissan Altima for $8700, how do you know what the price should be? One way is to look at the NADA or KBB.com site and see what the retail for that car is.

But a better way is to do an online search in your area on Google and see who else is selling similar cars and for how much. Once you have a range, price yours accordingly while keeping in mind your car's mileage.

Does color matter?

It does. Try not to buy any unusual colors at first, especially if you are only carrying 2-4 cars. Stay away from green purple and any unusual colors. Even though there is a demand for these odd colors but it is not enough for you to carry one of those colors unless you have 100 cars on your lot. Try to stay with neutral colors like silver, gray, blue, even red is okay, and remember lately black is becoming very popular too. I usually try not to carry too many white cars as they are boring to me, but that is just a personal choice.

Should You Buy from Auction or buy from other sources?

As you are getting started, I think you should get started the right way and buy from a reputable auction house. This way you know what you are buying and know you are paying the wholesale price for it. But when bidding, make sure you know ahead of time what is the max you can afford to pay for a particular vehicle. Do your research early, this way you will not lose money on any cars.

COMMONLY USED CAR DEALER TERMS

A

Absolute Auction – An auction where every vehicle is sold to the highest bidder.

Absolute Low – The lowest price a seller is willing to take for a vehicle.

Absolute Sale – (See Absolute Auction)

Acquisition Fee – A charge included in most lease transactions that is either paid up front or included in the total cost of the vehicle. This fee covers a variety of administrative costs, such as the costs of obtaining a credit report, verifying insurance coverage, checking the accuracy and completeness of the lease documentation and entering the lease into data and accounting systems.

Adjusted Capitalized Cost (Adjusted Cap Cost) – The amount capitalized at the beginning of the lease, equal to the gross capitalized cost. This amount is sometimes referred to as the net cap cost.

Arbitration – A service provided by the auctions to protect the interests of both buyers and sellers to insure the transaction has been properly represented.

Arena – The area where the auctioneer works and the vehicles are offered for sale. (Also called Ring)

"As Is" – (See Red Light) Specifics on what constitutes an "as is" vehicle can vary from one auction to another, but generally will include vehicles six years or older, with more than 100,000 miles registered on the odometer or where the odometer is suspect. Other factors affecting the evaluation of a vehicle may also apply, depending on the individual auction's policy.

At-Risk Vehicles – Cars or trucks owned by a daily rental company which, at their end of service, must be remarketed by the rental company. "Risk" means the rental company bears the risk of the price they will receive for this vehicle when it is retired from service. (Term "nonprogram vehicles" is preferred.)

Auction – The sale process by which multiple bidders compete to acquire a vehicle that is ultimately sold to the person offering the highest price.

Auctioneer – Highly skilled manager of the auction activity at the time of sale. Sometimes referred to as the "bid caller."

Auction Access – (See Dealer Registration) The national dealer registration system at some NAAA member auctions, which allows a dealer to electronically register at an auction and reserve a bidder badge. The system allows them to be automatically pre-registered at any participating member auction location.

Auction Agreement – A contract executed by the auction and its buyers and sellers that authorizes the auction to conduct the sale and sets out the terms of the agreement and the rights and responsibilities of each party.

Auction Guarantee – Specific guarantees may vary from one auction to the next, but usually cover the drivetrain, including (but not necessarily limited to) the engine, transmission and rear end.

Auction with Reserve – An auction where the sellers set a minimum price on their vehicles. They do not have to sell their vehicles if bidding fails to reach the reserve price, which may or may not be made public. (Floor price)

B

Bid – The amount of money offered for a vehicle in the sale.

Bid Assistants/Consultants/Spotters – (See Ringmen)

Bidder Badge – A credential that indicates a buyer's bidder number for a specific sale. The buyer is registered with Auction Access, and the bidder number is connected to the buyer's Auction Access account.

Bidder Number – The number issued to each qualified buyer on sale day.

Bill of Sale – A document provided by a seller showing the name of the purchaser and purchase price, which becomes the basis for calculation of sales and other taxes.

Black Book – Wholesale prices guide.

Block – The auctioneering and business transaction station in each auction lane.

Block Clerk – The person who records transaction information in the lanes.

Block Ticket – A computer-printed "paper trail" generated by the auction that documents the auction process from registration through the sale. (Also known as an invoice)

Buyer's Fee – A fee paid to the auction house by the winning bidder. The amount of the fee varies by auction.

C

Capitalized Cost (Cap Cost) – The price a buyer agrees to pay for a leased vehicle. The monthly lease payment is based on its depreciation, interest, administration, etc.

Capitalized Cost Reduction – An initial payment on a leased vehicle, which then lowers the monthly lease payment. That payment can consist of cash, a trade-in allowance on an existing vehicle or rebates and incentives provided by the manufacturer. The adjusted cap is the gross cap cost less the capitalized cost reduction.

Captive Finance Company – A leasing or finance company that is affiliated with a vehicle manufacturer.

Certificate of Origin – A document that conveys the title of a vehicle from the manufacturer to the dealer.

Closed Auction (sale) – An auction sale limited to

select dealers, such as those representing a particular franchise.

Closed-End Lease – A lease in which the lessee is not responsible for any difference between the actual and estimated residual value at the time of lease maturity. The lessee's only extra obligations under a closed end lease might be mileage or wear and tear exceeding the lease contract provisions.

Consignment – Vehicles assigned to an auction for sale.

Consignor – Any member of the remarketing community who provides vehicles for sale at the auction. Consignors range from automakers selling program cars to rental and corporate fleet operators to individual dealers.

Cross-Line Buying – Buying "across" manufacturer product lines, e.g., a Pontiac dealer buying a Cadillac at auction.

CyberLots® – Web-based collections of used vehicles that are offered to dealers for purchase over the Internet at a set price.

D

Daily Rental – Companies that rent cars by the day

or week.

Dealer – An individual who has been licensed by the state to transact the sale and purchase of new or used vehicles.

Dealer Invoice – The purchase price of the vehicle that the dealer is obliged to pay the manufacturer.

Dealer Registration – (See Auction Access) The procedure whereby licensed dealers are registered to do business at an auction.

Dealer Sale Representative – An individual designated to act on the dealer's behalf at wholesale auctions.

De-fleet – Action taken by commercial or rental fleet operators to reduce their number of vehicles.

Depreciation – The value lost as the vehicle ages. Depreciation is usually rapid in the early years of the vehicle's life and can be greater or less than the average because of mileage and wear and tear.

Depreciation and Any Amortized Amounts – Total amount charged to cover the vehicle's projected decline in value through normal use during the lease term, as well as other items that are paid for over the lease term. It is calculated as the difference between the adjusted capitalized cost and the vehicle's value at the end of the lease. This amount is a major part of a lessee's base monthly payment.

Disabled Sale – Auction term for a sale running inoperable vehicles with excess wear and tear.

Dispose, Resale, Remarket – Terms used to describe offering a titled vehicle for sale at an auction.

Draft – A bank collection item drawn by one bank on another. At auctions, the draft is signed by the buyer at the auction house and deposited, along with the title to the vehicle, in the auction's bank. After the auction's bank has collected from the buyer's bank, the title is released to the buyer.

E

Equity – In an installment sale or loan, the positive difference between the trade-in or market value of your vehicle and the loan payoff amount. When the loan is paid off, the equity is the market value of the vehicle.

Excess Mileage Charge – A charge by the lessor or assignee for miles driven in excess of the maximum specified in the lease agreement. The excess mileage charge is usually between $0.10 and $0.25 per mile. Suppose, for example, that your lease specifies a maximum of 36,000 miles and a charge of $0.15 per mile over the maximum. If you drive 37,000 miles, the excess mileage charge will be $0.15 x 1,000, or $150.

Excess Wear and Tear Charge – Amount charged by a lessor or assignee to cover wear and tear on a leased vehicle beyond what is considered normal. The charge may cover both interior and exterior damage, such as upholstery stains, body dents and scrapes and tire wear beyond the limits stated in the lease agreement.

Exotic Highline® – (See Highline) A Manheim-trademarked term for a rare, unique or top-of-the-line vehicle, typically in the sports or luxury segment.

F

Factory Sale – The same as closed sale in which buyers are limited to those representing a particular brand.

Fair Market Value – The current value of a particular vehicle in the marketplace, based on mileage, exterior and interior condition, mechanical fitness and such. Floorplanning – A dealer's vehicle inventory line of credit. Manheim Automotive Financial Services (MAFS®) specializes in dealer floorplanning through auctions.

Floor Price – The seller's asking price for a vehicle.

Frame Damage – Any damage to the frame or frame members of a vehicle. Refer also to the NAAA Frame Policy.

Franchised Dealer – A licensed vehicle dealer authorized to sell and service a specific brand of new vehicles.

Frontline Ready – Vehicles that are in retail-ready condition and ready to be put in the front line of a dealer's lot.

G

Green Light – Auction term for a vehicle that is sold with some buyer protection as to its condition.

Gross Capitalized Cost (Gross Cap Cost) – The agreed-upon value of the vehicle, which generally may be negotiated, plus any items the lessee agrees to pay for over the lease term (amortized amounts), such as taxes, fees, service contracts, insurance and any prior credit or lease balance.

H

Hammer Falls – An expression used to indicate that the auctioneer has struck a deal between the buyer and the seller, and a sale is consummated.

Hammer Price – The price offered by the last bidder and accepted by the auctioneer, who bangs the hammer or gavel to acknowledge this price as the sale price.

Heavy Truck – Trucks with a Gross Vehicle Weight over 33,000 lbs. are Class 8 or Heavy Duty. Class 7 trucks, 26,000 to 33,000 Gross Vehicle Weight are sometimes referred to as Heavy Duty.

Highline® – (See Exotic Highline) Manheim-trademarked term for a top-of-the-line car.

I

IF – An offer made strictly between the buyer and the seller and not binding on either party until the sale is consummated. Usually facilitated by the auction between the buyer and seller. The bidder agrees to buy the vehicle "IF" the seller will accept the offer within a specified period of time.

Incentives – A form of reward offered to boost sales; a special price reduction or rebate from vehicle manufacturers to influence the sale of a particular model. Incentives can be low to zero percent financing rates, no down payment, cash back offers, "free" options, etc.

Independent Dealer – A used vehicle dealer who is not associated with a manufacturer.

Inventory Turn – A measure of a dealer's operations that calculates how quickly he sells, or "turns," his inventory.

K

Kelley Blue Book – A publication that lists prices of used vehicles.

L

Lane – The passageway in front of the auctioneer where the vehicle travels to the block to be offered for sale. Usually listed as Lane 1, 2, 3, etc. or Lane A, B, C, etc.

Lease – A contract between a lessor and a lessee for the use of a vehicle or other property, subject to stated terms and limitations, for a specified period and at a specified payment.

Lessee – The company or individual to whom a vehicle is leased.

Lessor – The party to a lease agreement who holds legal or tax title to the vehicle and receives the lease payments.

Lights – (See Blue, Green, Yellow, Red) Each color provides important information about the condition of a vehicle, and is illuminated while bidding is underway.

Light Truck – A truck under 16,000 Gross Vehicle Weight, including pickups and vans. Classes 1 to 3.

M

Manufacturer's Statement of Origin (MSO) – (See Certificate of Origin)

Manufacturer's Suggested Retail Price (MSRP) – The suggested retail price the dealer is asking. Generally the same as the "sticker price."

N

National Automobile Auction Association (NAAA) – An international organization whose members operate wholesale vehicle auctions. NAAA's 360 member auctions remarket more than 16 million vehicles annually and are active in the Americas,

Europe, Asia, Australia and New Zealand.

National Automobile Dealers Association (NADA) – Founded in 1917, NADA represents more than 19,400 franchised vehicle dealers.

National Association of Fleet Administrators (NAFA) – A professional organization created in 1957 for automotive fleet managers.

National independent Automobile Dealers Association (NIADA) – Formed in 1946 to represent independent automobile dealers nationwide.

No Sale Fee – A fee charged by the auction to the seller when a vehicle goes through the lane but is not sold.

O

Online Auction – An auction held over the Internet.

Open Auction – A wholesale auction open to all licensed car dealers, both franchised and independent.

Open-End Lease – A lease where no specific time limit is set for the vehicle to remain in service. In most cases, at the end of the lease, any gain or loss from the sale of the vehicle belongs to the lessee.

P

Post-Sale Inspection – An inspection service that helps dealers ensure that a purchased vehicle meets its announced conditions. Auction personnel test drive the car and inspect its frame and mechanical condition to ensure quality and performance before sending it on to the dealer's lot.

Program Car – A vehicle that is sold directly to a daily rental company by an automaker under terms set by the manufacturer. Program cars represent a large portion of current model-year vehicles remarketed through auctions.

Private Transaction – When one consumer sells a vehicle to another consumer without the interaction of a car dealer.

R

Reconditioning (Recon) – The process of correcting mechanical and cosmetic defects to prepare a vehicle for resale. Auctions typically provide these services to consignors because their investments are more than fullly recovered through the lanes.

Red Light – Indicates a vehicle being sold "As Is." A

red light is illuminated while bidding is underway on such a vehicle.

Remarketing – The term that encompasses all services as well as the actual transfer of a vehicle from seller to buyer.

Resale, Remarket, Dispose – Terms used to describe offering a titled vehicle for sale at an auction.

Reserve Price – In most cases, the minimum price a seller is willing to accept.

Residual (Value) – The projection of the market value of a vehicle at the end of a lease. Specialized companies that evaluate used car price data to make their forecasts typically calculate residual values. Financial companies, including the captive finance operations of the auto companies, use these values to set lease terms.

Retail Price – The price paid by a consumer to a dealer or individual for a vehicle. The dealer or individual sets the retail price of a used car by evaluating the wholesale price paid plus reconditioning expense and other costs.

Retail Transaction – When a licensed car dealer sells a new or used car to a private individual. It is estimated that there are 1.6 wholesale transactions supporting every retail transaction.

Ring – (See Arena) The area where the auctioneer works and the vehicles are offered for sale.

Risk or At-Risk Vehicles – Cars or trucks owned by a daily rental company, which, at their end of service, must be disposed of by the rental company. "Risk" refers to the fact that the rental company is responsible for remarketing these vehicles at the end of their rental service, and thereby they are taking the price risk. By contrast, program cars are sold to rental companies with end-of-service price guarantees.

Run List – The listing of vehicles for sale at a particular auction.

Run Numbers – (a) Numbers assigned to a vehicle or a consignors' group of vehicles when lane reservations are made. (b) Position in the lane during an auction.

S

Salvage – A vehicle that is not economical to repair and is sold for the value of its salvageable parts.

Seller's Market – A market in which all or certain

vehicles are scarce, and therefore buyers have a limited selection and prices usually tend to be high.

Seller's Fee (Sale Fee) – The fee paid by the seller to the auction after the vehicle is sold. The fee usually is based on the sale price of the vehicle.

Simulcast Auction – A live auction that is simultaneously transmitted to remote locations via the Internet so that dealers not physically at an auction can bid in real time for vehicles in the lanes.

Subvention – A program or plan in which certain items are subsidized by the manufacturer, the finance company, the lessor or the assignee.

SUV – Sport Utility Vehicle.

T

Title – A legal document issued by the state showing the owner's name and the vehicle's mileage at the time of sale.

"Title Absent" (or "Title Attached")

Transactions – When a vehicle is sold "title absent," the title is not available on auction day and must be produced and delivered to the auction by the seller within a certain period of time.

Trade-in – A vehicle that is sold to either a new or used car dealer as part of the purchase of another.

U

Unit – A single car or truck. A dealer's or an auction's fleet operator, or a rental company's volume, is expressed in number of units.

Used Car Guidebooks – Publications that report current wholesale and/or retail prices of vehicles. Wholesale values generally are determined from factors including auto auction prices, other wholesale transactions and regional demand. Prices are listed according to year, make, model, options, mileage and condition of the vehicle. Retail prices generally are determined by factors including dealership retail sales prices, other retail transactions and regional demand.

V

Vehicle Identification Number (VIN) – A 17-digit combination of letters and numbers that identifies an individual vehicle. It is located on the driver's side of the dashboard at the base where the windshield glass and dashboard meet. Each digit or letter in the VIN provides information about the vehicle.

W

Wholesale Price – The price paid for a vehicle by a purchaser who intends to resell the vehicle.

Wholesaler – A dealer who buys vehicles at auction – or from a dealer or another wholesaler – and resells them in the wholesale market, i.e., to dealers rather than consumers. Wholesalers also buy and sell cars among the dealers with whom they do business.

Y

Yellow Light – A vehicle that is being offered with certain conditions that are announced prior to sale. Buyers cannot take these conditions to arbitration. A yellow light is illuminated while bidding is underway on such a vehicle.

(Courtesy of www.NAAA.com A great resource for everything auto auction)

LAST WORDS

HOPEFULLY, in this book, I was able to give you a good general overview of the used car dealership business. Remember to follow the direction and guidelines I provided here, it will take some effort, some leg work, and some money but it is doable and a truly easy to run business. Remember, if you buy the right cars, they will sell themselves.

I wanted to thank you for buying my book; I am neither a professional writer nor an author, but rather a person who always had the passion for cars and car business. In this book, I wanted to share my knowledge with you, as I know many people share the same passion and drive as I do. So, this book is entirely dedicated to you.

Despite my best effort to make this book error free, if you happen to find any errors, I want to ask for your forgiveness ahead of time.

Just remember, my writing skills may not be best, but the knowledge I share here is pure and honest.

If you thought I added some value and shared some valuable information that you can use, please take a minute and post a review on wherever you bought this book from. This will mean the world to me. Thank you so much!!

Lastly, I wanted to thank my wife Jill and my dear friend Jacob for all their help and support throughout this book, without them, this book would not have been possible.

If you need to get in touch with me for any reason, please feel free to email me at valenciapublishing@gmail.com

Thank you once again and good luck on your new business venture.

www.ingramcontent.com/pod-product-compliance
Lightning Source LLC
Chambersburg PA
CBHW071443180526
45170CB00001B/445